Also by White Barn Press

*Vintage Garden Ephemera*

*Vintage Ephemera Sampler*

*Vintage Bird Ephemera*

Copyright © 2021

All rights reserved.

See their Eyes, as she buys FRY'S.

Vintage advertising was truly a work of art! This edition of vintage advertising ephemera is full of so many beautiful examples of advertising art from the mid 19th through the early 20th century. The oldest featured here are the Schmidt Litho Company (Apple Labels) from 1825 and Harrison's Handkerchief Extracts from 1854. Also included, Huyler's Cocoa and Chocolate, a candy and restaurant chain in New York City from 1874 to 1964. Can you imagine the sights and sounds you may have experienced as you enjoyed this cup of hot cocoa in New York City at the turn of the 20th century?  Also found in this collection, the Hecker Jones Jewell Milling Company famous for developing the first self rising flour and winning gold medals at the 1851 World's fair in London. So many wonderful vintage pieces can be found in this collection. It is my hope that they bring much joy to your creations!

*Maggie Ray Fields*
White Barn Press

The TRUE ELIXIR OF LIFE

BOVININE

BOVININE

The GREAT TONIC and RESTORATIVE FLUID FOOD

For OVER-WORKED and INSUFFICIENTLY NOURISHED PEOPLE.

Overtaxed professional and laboring men.

EXHAUSTED MOTHERS. Sickly and feeble infants and OLD AGE Children. is rendered comfortable and enjoyable by its daily use.

PRESCRIBED By Physicians all over the UNION.

The J.P. BUSH MFG. CO. Chicago & New York. N.Y. OFFICE 2 Barclay St. N.Y.

Picture of a young Child whose Life was saved by BOVININE.

OVER

FERNANDO B. SMITH'S. PATENT SPRINKLER AND NOVELTY FORCE PUMP. CANTON. OHIO. U.S.A.

F. WIMMER AERATED WATER & CORDIAL MANUFACTURER

LEMONADE

QUALITY DRINKS PHONE 32 NAMBOUR

BACK ACHE QUICKLY RELIEVED BY CARTER'S Smart Weed & Belladonna BACK ACHE PLASTERS

WEMPLE & COMPANY NEW YORK.

SEE OTHER SIDE

ASK FOR THURBERS' CANNED BALDWIN TOMATOES, LIMA BEANS, STRINGLESS BEANS, WINDHAM CORN, MARROW & LA FAVORITA PEAS, OKRA & TOMATOES, SUCCOTASH, ETC. ETC.

The Baldwin

SEE OVER

SCHMIDLAPP'S LIVE OAK DISTILLERY.

Fine copper distilled BOURBON WHISKY

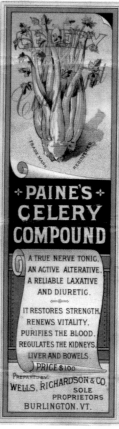

MARSEILLES WHITE SOAP.

A LAUNDRY SOAP CONTAINING ALL THE QUALITIES OF THE FINEST TOILET & BATH SOAP.

Marseilles WHITE SOAP.

WILL NOT SHRINK YOUR WOOLENS OR FLANNELS.

MADE BY Lautz Bros. & Co. Buffalo. N.Y.

FOR LIST OF PREMIUMS SEE BACK OF OUTSIDE WRAPPER.

Use Pyle's Pearline

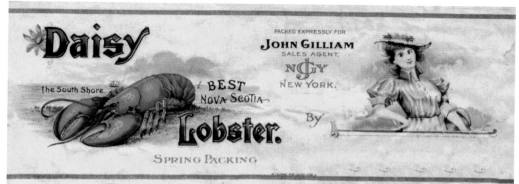

Daisy

The South Shore

BEST NOVA SCOTIA Lobster.

SPRING PACKING

PACKED EXPRESSLY FOR JOHN GILLIAM SALES AGENT, N.Y. CITY NEW YORK.

By

KING BEE

IT'S EQUAL NEVER SEEN.

SWEET and PLEASANT.

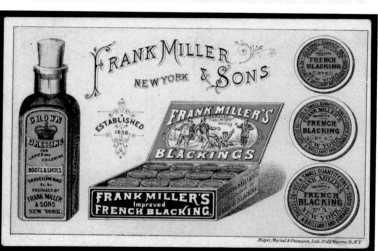

FRANK MILLER & SONS NEW YORK

ESTABLISHED 1838.

FRANK MILLER'S BLACKINGS

FRANK MILLER'S Improved FRENCH BLACKING.

CROWN DRESSING FOR LADIES and CHILDRENS BOOTS & SHOES TRAVELLING BAGS &c &c PREPARED BY FRANK MILLER & SONS NEW YORK

MARSEILLES WHITE SOAP.

Marseilles WHITE SOAP. Lautz Bros & Co BUFFALO N.Y.

Mama says this is better MADE SOLID AND LASTS LONGER WILL NOT SHRINK YOUR WOOLENS OR FLANNELS

FOR LIST OF PREMIUMS SEE BACK OF OUTSIDE WRAPPER.

COPYRIGHT 1898 BY JOSEPH F KNAPP.

THE KNAPP CO. LITHO. N.Y.

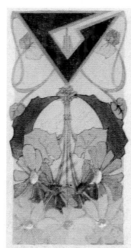

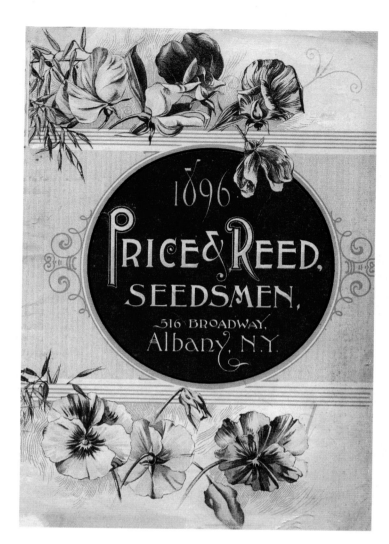

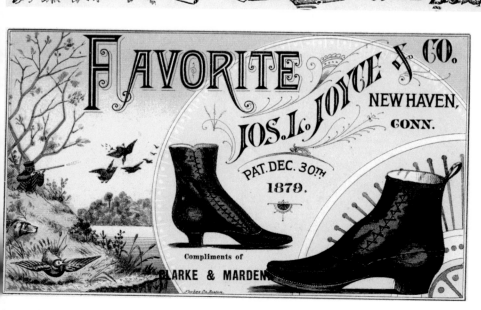

I always drink *Huyler's* Cocoa or Chocolate!

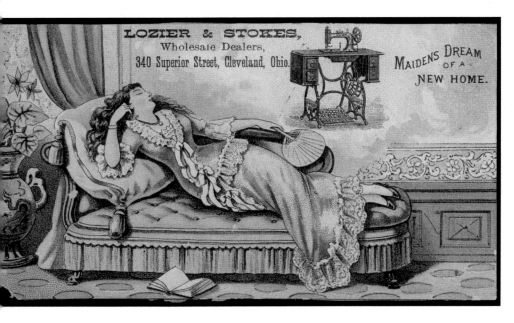

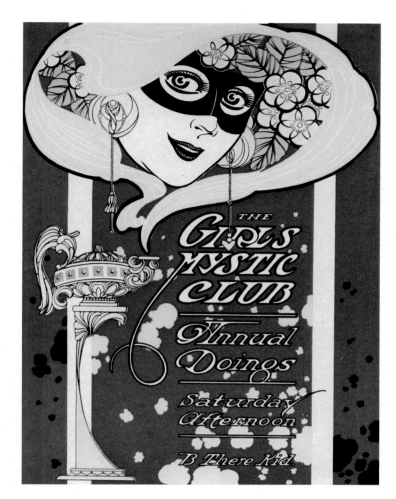

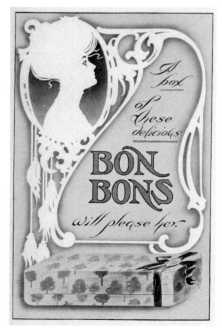

KING GEORGE IV. SCOTCH WHISKY

J.C. WILLIAMSON'S GORGEOUS ANNUAL PANTOMIME.

GOODY TWO SHOES

THE TOP-NOTCH OF SCOTCH

MANUFACTURE AND HAVE FOR SALE:

CHOCOLATE
HOMEOPATHIC
FELL & SON'S EXTRA
CLAY & CO'S EXTRA
COURTLAND N°1
W.OAK & CO. N°1
ALBERT N° 1
NAGLE N° 1
SWEET SPANISH
VANILLA SWEET

COCOA
PREPARED
SOLUBLE
CRACKED
COCOA PASTE
COCOA SHELLS

BROMA

C.J. FELL & BROTHER
54 S.th FRONT ST. PHILADELPHIA

MUSTARD
SUPERFINE
FINE
ENGLISH
BROWN
CLAY & CO.

PEPPER
PURE GROUND
N° 1 GROUND
SUPERIOR GROUND
PURE GROUND AFRICAN
CAYENNE
PURE GROUND AMERICAN
CAYENNE

GINGER
PURE & N°1
CALCUTTA
D. AFRICAN
WHOLE & GROUND
JAMAICA

PURE & N°1 GROUND
CINNAMON
ALLSPICE
CLOVES
PURE GROUND
NUTMEGS
MACE
PURE
RICE FLOUR
HOMINY
GRITS
BARLEY
BAKING P°S.
STARCH POLISH
SALARATUS

Transpose the initials of these flowers names so as to form a word which has been the basis of the Success of

Solution of this problem is every package. AM. BALL BLUE

AMERICAN BALL BLUE

HELLER & MERZ.
NEW YORK.

HEATHERBLOOM
TAFFETA

PETTICOATS

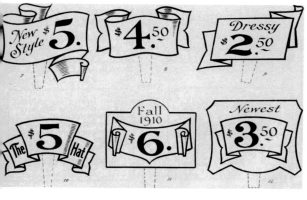

New Style $5.
$4.50
Dressy $2.50
The $5 Hat
Fall 1910 $6.
Newest $3.50

Select Styles
►1910◄

YEAST FOAM
RECIPES

"MANCHESTER"

DIXON'S
CARBURET
OF IRON
STOVE
POLISH

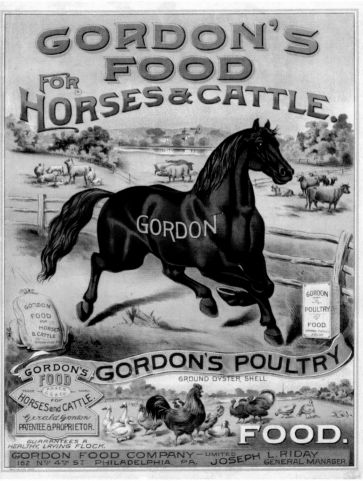

GORDON'S FOOD
FOR HORSES & CATTLE

GORDON

GORDON'S POULTRY FOOD.

USE
KIDDS COUGH SYRUP
SAFE FOR CHILDREN
PRICE
ONLY 25 CENTS.
Prepared by
FLEMING BROS.
PITTSBURGH.
PA.

PERFUMED WITH
AUSTEN'S
FOREST FLOWER COLOGNE

W. J. AUSTEN & CO.
OSWEGO, N.Y. OVER

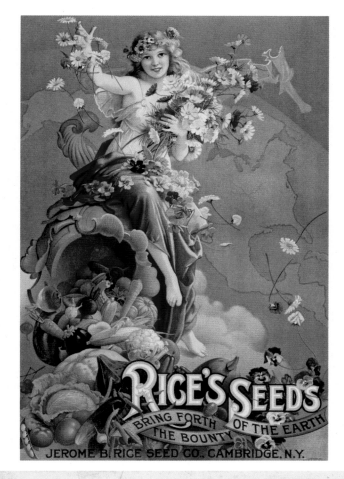

RICE'S SEEDS
BRING FORTH OF THE EARTH
THE BOUNTY

JEROME B. RICE SEED CO. CAMBRIDGE, N.Y.

Armant's
Perfumes

Herman Loeb & Co. N.Y.

HARRISON'S HANDKERCHIEF EXTRACTS

RICE & CO.,
Dealers in
DRUGS, MEDICINES,
and Choice Toilet Goods,
No. 5 Lincklaen Street,
CAZENOVIA, N.Y.

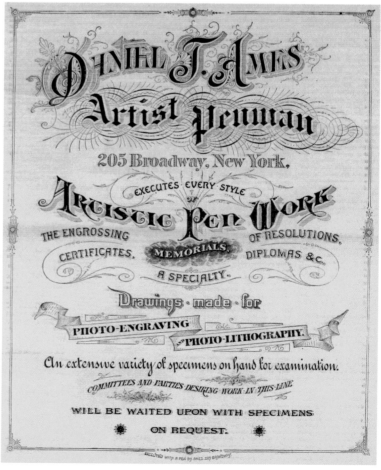

# Acknowledgements

C. J. Fell & Brother 64 Sth. Front St. Philadelphia, 1866-1872, priJLC_FOOD_001979, Jay T. Last Collection of Graphic Arts and Social History, The Huntington Library, San Marino, California

Schmidlapp's live oak distillery, 1872, priJLC_BEV_001866, Jay T. Last Collection of Graphic Arts and Social History, The Huntington Library, San Marino, California

Rice's seeds bring forth the bounty of the earth, 1921, priJLC_HORT_002467, Jay T. Last Collection of Graphic Arts and Social History, The Huntington Library, San Marino, California

Made in the USA
Monee, IL
15 December 2021

85740610R00024